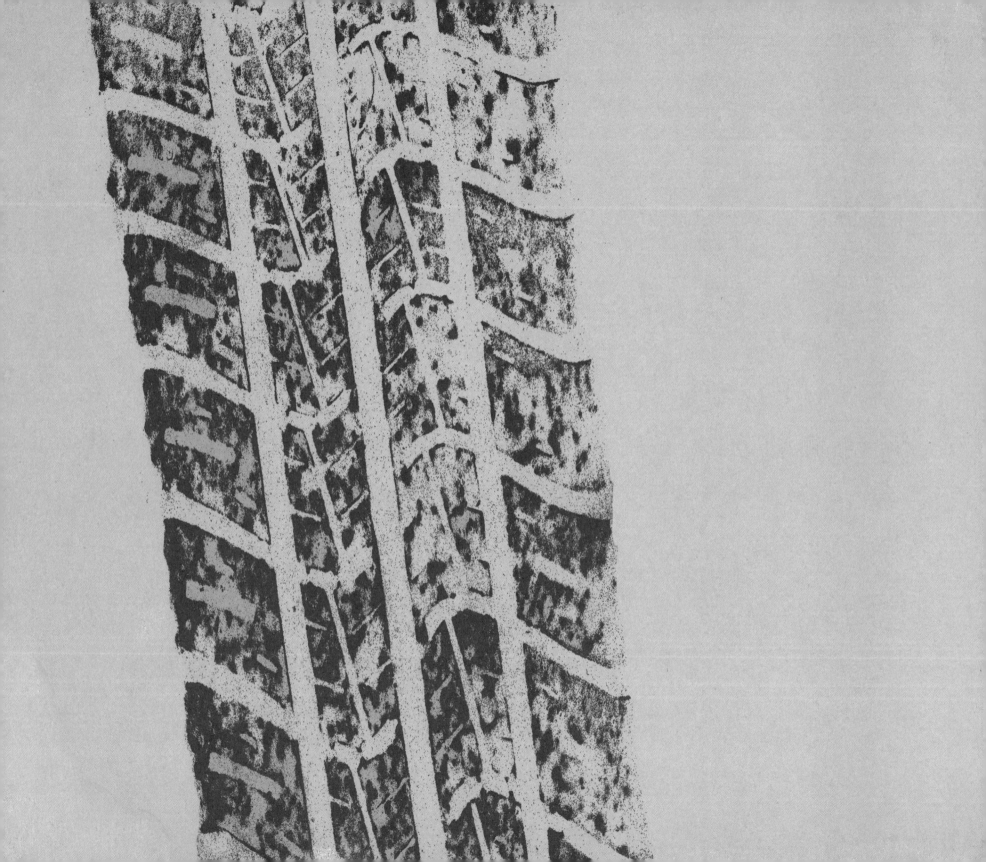

I DRIVE A CRANE

by **Sarah Bridges**

illustrated by **Amy Bailey Muehlenhardt**

PICTURE WINDOW BOOKS
Minneapolis, Minnesota

Thanks to Bill Barnes of the City of Minneapolis
for all of the great stories. S.B.

Editor: Jill Kalz
Designer: Jaime Martens
Page Production: Tracy Kaehler,
Brandie Shoemaker, Zachary Trover
Creative Director: Keith Griffin
Editorial Director: Carol Jones
The illustrations in this book were created digitally.

Picture Window Books
5115 Excelsior Boulevard
Suite 232
Minneapolis, MN 55416
877-845-8392
www.picturewindowbooks.com

Printed in the United States of America.

Library of Congress Cataloging-in-Publication Data
Bridges, Sarah.
I drive a crane / by Sarah Bridges ; illustrated by Amy Bailey
Muehlenhardt.
p. cm. — (Working wheels)
Includes bibliographical references and index.
ISBN 1-4048-1605-4 (hardcover)
1. Cranes, derricks, etc.—Juvenile literature. I. Muehlenhardt,
Amy Bailey, 1974— II. Title.
TJ1363.B8175 2005
c22   2005023140

Thanks to our advisers for their expertise, research, and advice:

Rod Sutton, Editor in Chief, and Walt Moore, Senior Editor
Construction Equipment Magazine, Oak Brook, Illinois

Susan Kesselring, M.A., Literacy Educator
Rosemount–Apple Valley–Eagan (Minnesota) School District

My name is Peter. I drive a tower crane. My crane lifts things that are too heavy or awkward for other machines to lift. It is taller than a 15-story building.

Workers put tower cranes together at the start of a job and take them apart when a job is done.

5

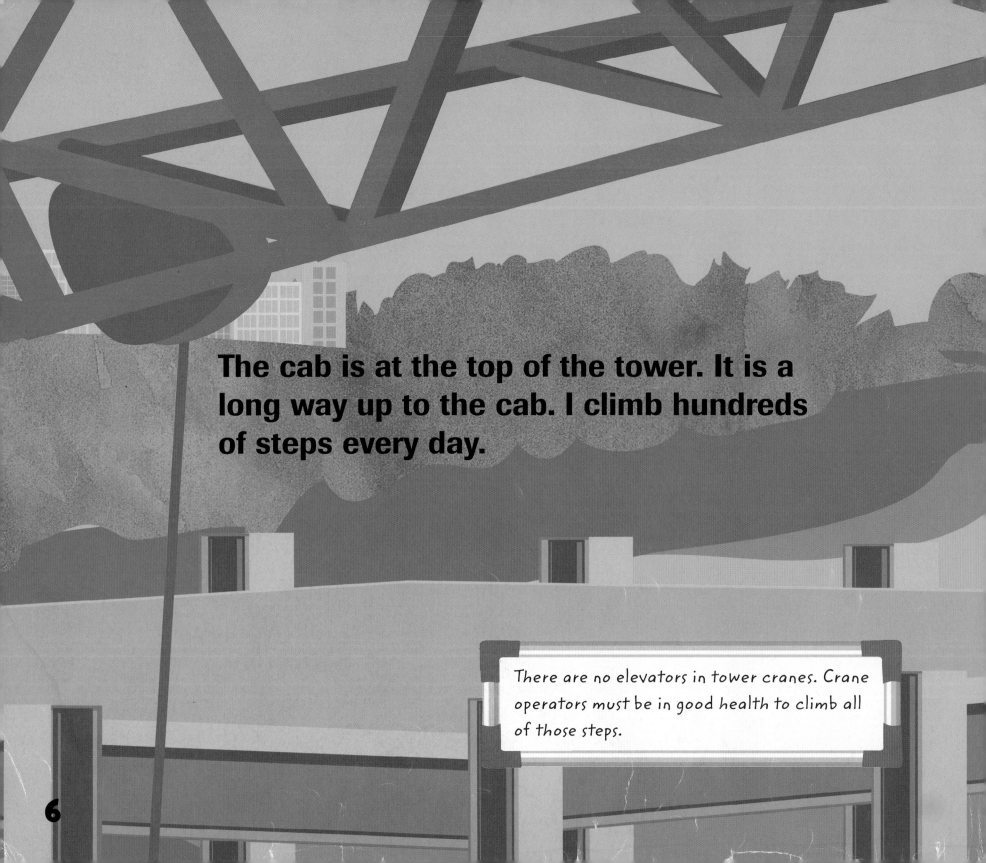

The cab is at the top of the tower. It is a long way up to the cab. I climb hundreds of steps every day.

There are no elevators in tower cranes. Crane operators must be in good health to climb all of those steps.

The cab is very small. It has a driver's seat, dials, and levers. Dials show how high loads are being lifted. They also show how well the crane's motors are running.

A crane operator uses a set of levers to lift loads, carry them to the correct spots, and lower them again.

9

The wind outside the cab whistles loudly. Even though my crane is bolted down to a concrete pad, it sways with the breeze.

Tower cranes are made to sway in strong winds. If they weren't able to sway, a big gust of wind might snap them in two.

11

The beam above my head is called the boom. A trolley slides along one end. It moves the load. The other end of the boom holds concrete counterweights.

Without counterweights, a tower crane would tip over whenever it tried to lift something heavy.

13

I push a lever and lower the crane's cable and hook to the ground.

Cables are made of many metal ropes. There may be more than 100 ropes in each cable.

14

15

Before I lift a load, I place a test weight on the hook. I do this test to make sure the crane can handle the load.

16

It is impossible for tower crane operators to hear people on the ground. Operators must use two-way radios to communicate with other workers.

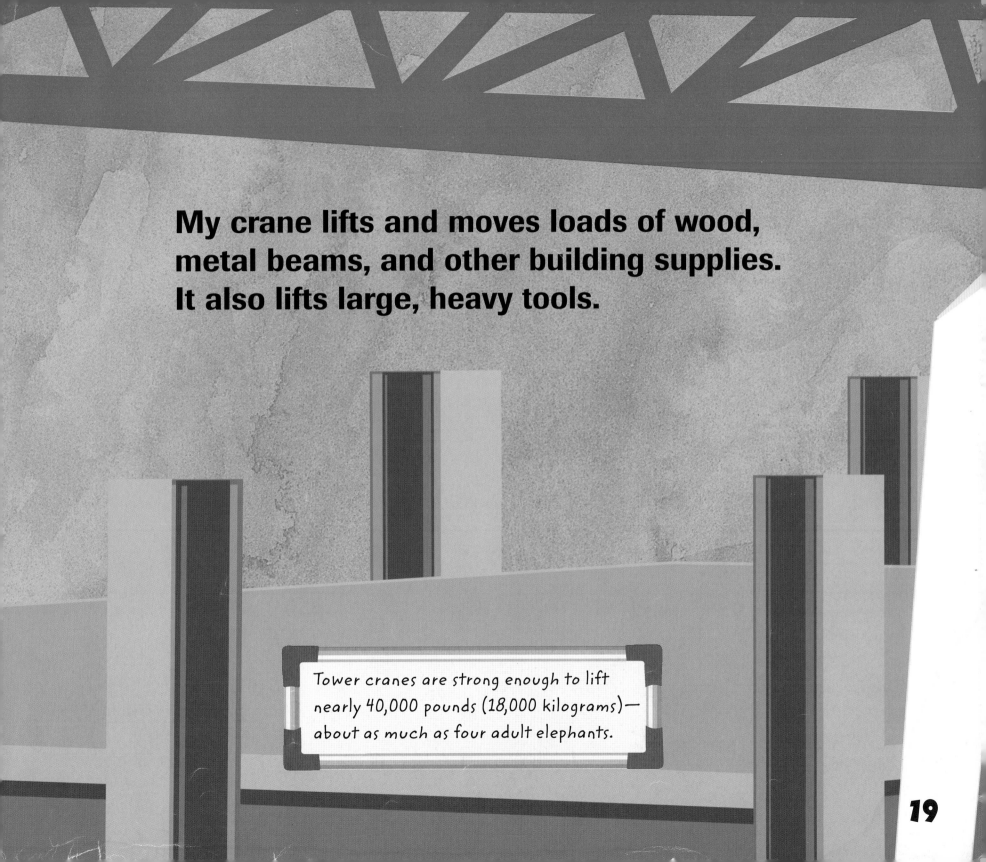

My crane lifts and moves loads of wood, metal beams, and other building supplies. It also lifts large, heavy tools.

Tower cranes are strong enough to lift nearly 40,000 pounds (18,000 kilograms)— about as much as four adult elephants.

When I am done for the day, I make sure the cab is locked for the night. Then I carefully climb back down to the ground.

Crane operators travel from one job to another. They may be away from home for long periods of time.

CRANE DIAGRAM

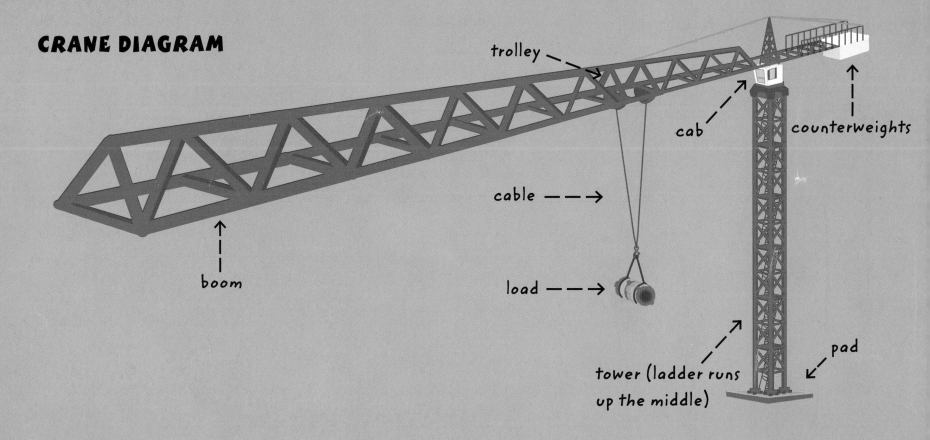

trolley

cab

counterweights

cable ‑ ‑ →

load ‑ ‑ →

boom

tower (ladder runs up the middle)

pad

GLOSSARY

beam—a long, usually square, piece of metal or wood

boom—the beam on top of a tower crane

cab—the place where the driver, or operator, of a crane sits

cables—thick, metal ropes

counterweights—concrete blocks used to balance a crane's load

operator—a person who is in control of a vehicle or machine

trolley—the sliding cart on a tower crane's boom that moves the load

FUN FACTS

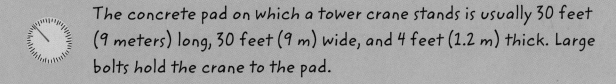 The concrete pad on which a tower crane stands is usually 30 feet (9 meters) long, 30 feet (9 m) wide, and 4 feet (1.2 m) thick. Large bolts hold the crane to the pad.

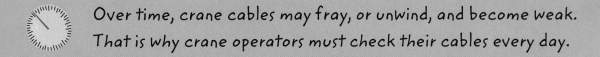 Over time, crane cables may fray, or unwind, and become weak. That is why crane operators must check their cables every day.

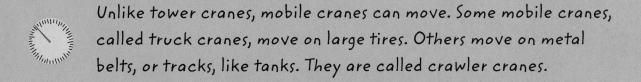 Unlike tower cranes, mobile cranes can move. Some mobile cranes, called truck cranes, move on large tires. Others move on metal belts, or tracks, like tanks. They are called crawler cranes.

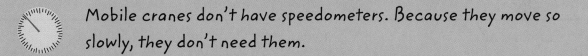 Mobile cranes don't have speedometers. Because they move so slowly, they don't need them.

TO LEARN MORE

At the Library

Ladd, Frances. *The Crane*. New York: Scholastic, 2003.

Star, Fleur. *Crane*. New York: DK Publishing, 2005.

Williams, Linda D. *Cranes*. Mankato, Minn.: Capstone Press, 2005.

On the Web

FactHound offers a safe, fun way to find Internet sites related to this book. All of the sites on FactHound have been researched by our staff.

1. Visit www.facthound.com

2. Type in this special code for age-appropriate sites: 1404816054

3. Click on the FETCH IT button.

Your trusty FactHound will fetch the best sites for you!

INDEX

LOOK FOR ALL OF THE BOOKS IN THE WORKING WHEELS SERIES:

- I Drive a Backhoe
  1-4048-1604-6
- I Drive a Bulldozer
  1-4048-0613-X
- I Drive a Crane
  1-4048-1605-4
- I Drive a Dump Truck
  1-4048-0614-8

- I Drive a Fire Engine
  1-4048-1606-2
- I Drive a Freight Train
  1-4048-1607-0
- I Drive a Garbage Truck
  1-4048-0615-6
- I Drive an Ambulance
  1-4048-0618-0

- I Drive a Semitruck
  1-4048-0616-4
- I Drive a Snowplow
  1-4048-0617-2
- I Drive a Street Sweeper
  1-4048-1608-9
- I Drive a Tractor
  1-4048-1609-7

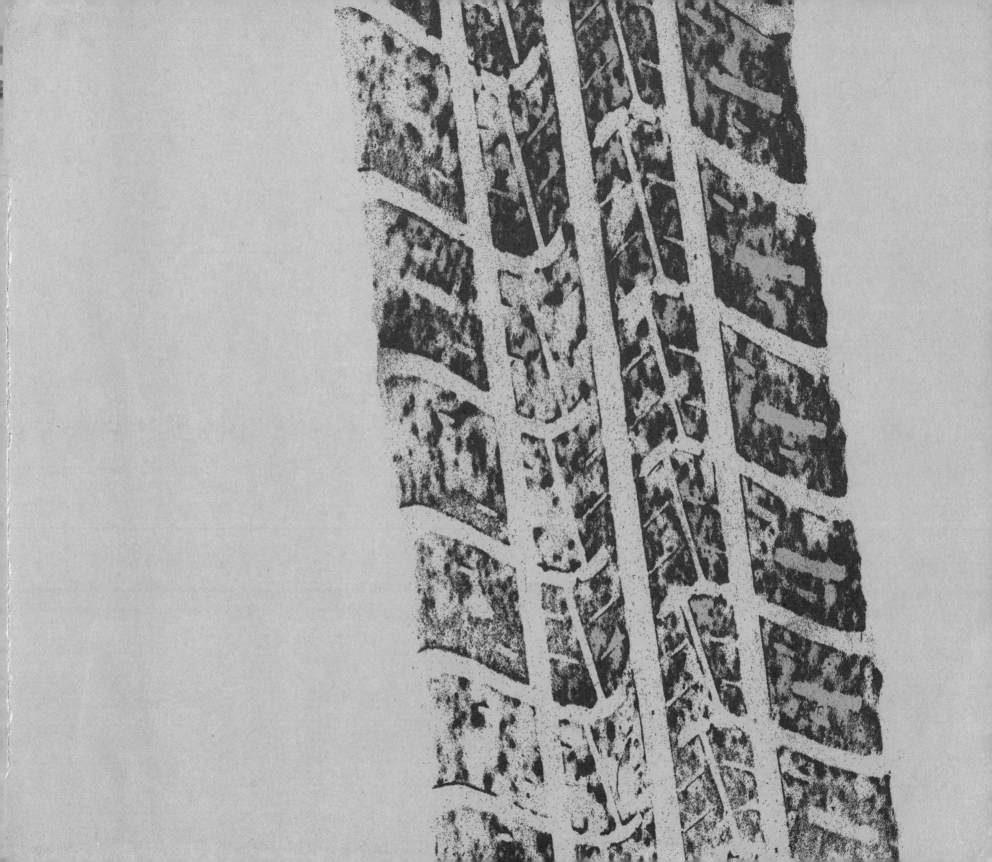